Pebble Bilingual Books

Soy honrado/
I Am Honest

de/by
Sarah L. Schuette

Traducción/Translation
Martín Luis Guzmán Ferrer, Ph.D.

Capstone Press
Mankato, Minnesota

Pebble Bilingual Books are published by Capstone Press
151 Good Counsel Drive, P.O. Box 669, Mankato, Minnesota 56002
http://www.capstone-press.com

1 2 3 4 5 6 08 07 06 05 04 03

Library of Congress Cataloging-in-Publication Data
Schuette, Sarah L., 1976–
[I am honest. Spanish & English]
Soy honrado / de Sarah L. Schuette; traducción, Martín Luis Guzmán Ferrer =
I am honest / by Sarah L. Schuette; translation, Martín Luis Guzmán Ferrer.
p. cm.—(Pebble bilingual books)
Spanish and English.
Includes index.
Summary: Simple text and photographs show various ways children can be
honest.
ISBN 0-7368-2303-4 (hardcover)
1. Honesty—Juvenile literature. [1. Honesty. 2. Spanish language materials—
Bilingual.] I. Title: I am honest. II. Title. III. Series: Pebble bilingual books.
BJ1533.H7S3818 2004
179′.9—dc21   2003004927

Credits
Mari C. Schuh and Martha E. H. Rustad, editors; Jennifer Schonborn, series designer
and illustrator; Patrick Dentinger, cover production designer; Gary Sundermeyer,
photographer; Nancy White, photo stylist; Karen Risch, product planning editor;
Eida Del Risco, Spanish copy editor; Gail Saunders-Smith, consulting editor;
Madonna Murphy, Ph.D., Professor of Education, University of St. Francis, Joliet,
Illinois, author of *Character Education in America's Blue Ribbon Schools*, consultant

Pebble Books thanks the Le family of Mankato, Minnesota, for modeling in this book.
The author dedicates this book to the memory of her grandparents, Willmar and
Janet Schuette, formerly of Belle Plaine, Minnesota.

Table of Contents

Contenido

I am honest. I tell the truth.

Yo soy honrado. Digo la verdad.

No food or
drink allowed
in the store

Thanks for your
cooperation
--Management

6

I am honest when I
follow the rules.

Soy honrado cuando
cumplo con las reglas.

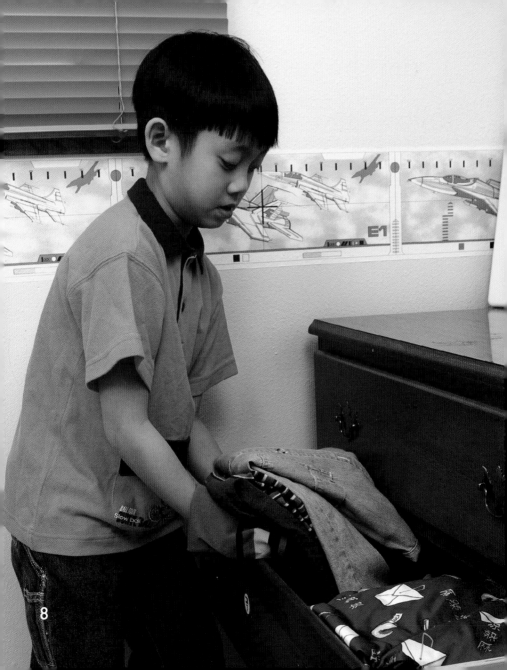

I am honest when I
do what I say I will do.

Soy honrado cuando
hago lo que digo
que voy a hacer.

I pay for the things I
want. I tell the clerk if
I get too much change.

Pago por las cosas
que quiero. Le aviso
a la dependienta si
me devuelve de más.

I do my own work.
I do not copy from
other people.

Hago mi propio trabajo.
No copio de los demás.

I tell my friend
if I break his things.

Le aviso a mi amigo
cuando rompo sus cosas.

I do not blame others
for my mistakes.

No le echo la culpa a
los demás de mis errores.

I am honest with
my parents. I tell
them when I am
afraid or upset.

Soy honrado con
mis padres. Les digo
cuando estoy
asustado o molesto.

I am honest. I tell the truth. People can trust me.

Yo soy honrado. Digo la verdad. La gente puede confiar en mí.

Glossary

blame—to hold yourself or someone else responsible for something that happened; people who are honest take responsibility for their own actions.

clerk—a person who sells things at a store

copy—to take another person's work and use it as your own

follow—to obey a rule; people are honest when they follow rules.

honest—to be truthful; people who are honest do not lie.

mistake—something that often happens by accident; people do not mean to make mistakes.

rule—an instruction telling people what to do; rules help people learn, stay healthy, and stay safe.

Glosario

culpable—aceptar que uno mismo u otra persona es responsable de algo que pasa; las personas honradas aceptan la responsabilidad de sus propios actos.

dependienta *(la)*—persona que vende cosas en la tienda

copiar—apropiarse del trabajo de otra persona y usarlo como si fuera de uno

cumplir—obedecer; las personas son honradas cuando cumplen con las reglas.

honrado—decir la verdad; las personas honradas no mienten.

error *(el)*—algo que frecuentemente sucede por accidente; no es la intención de las personas cometer errores.

regla—una instrucción que le dice a las personas qué hacer; las reglas ayudan a la gente a aprender, estar sana y segura.

Index

Índice